PZL-104
Wilga 35A

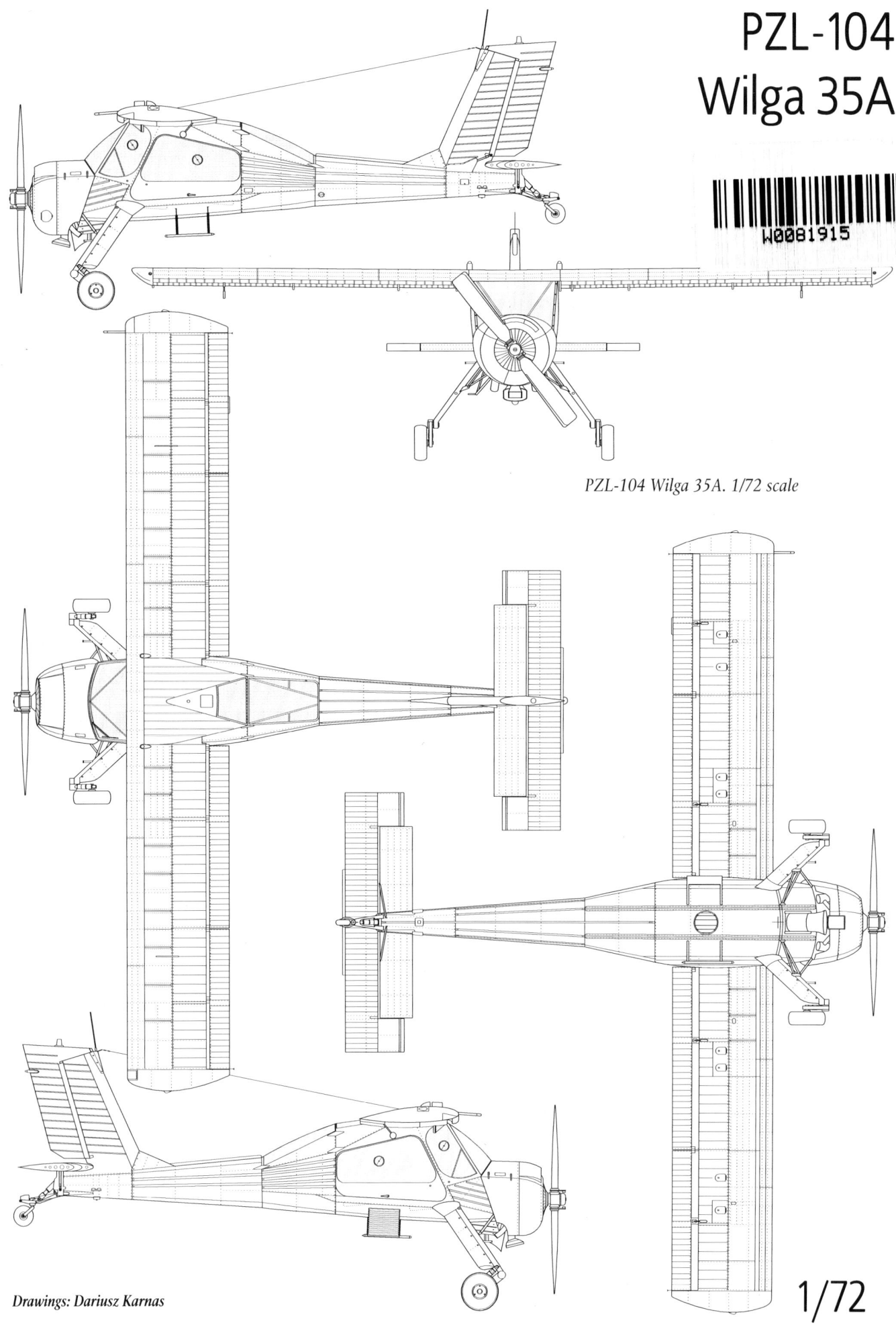

PZL-104 Wilga 35A. 1/72 scale

1/72

Drawings: Dariusz Karnas

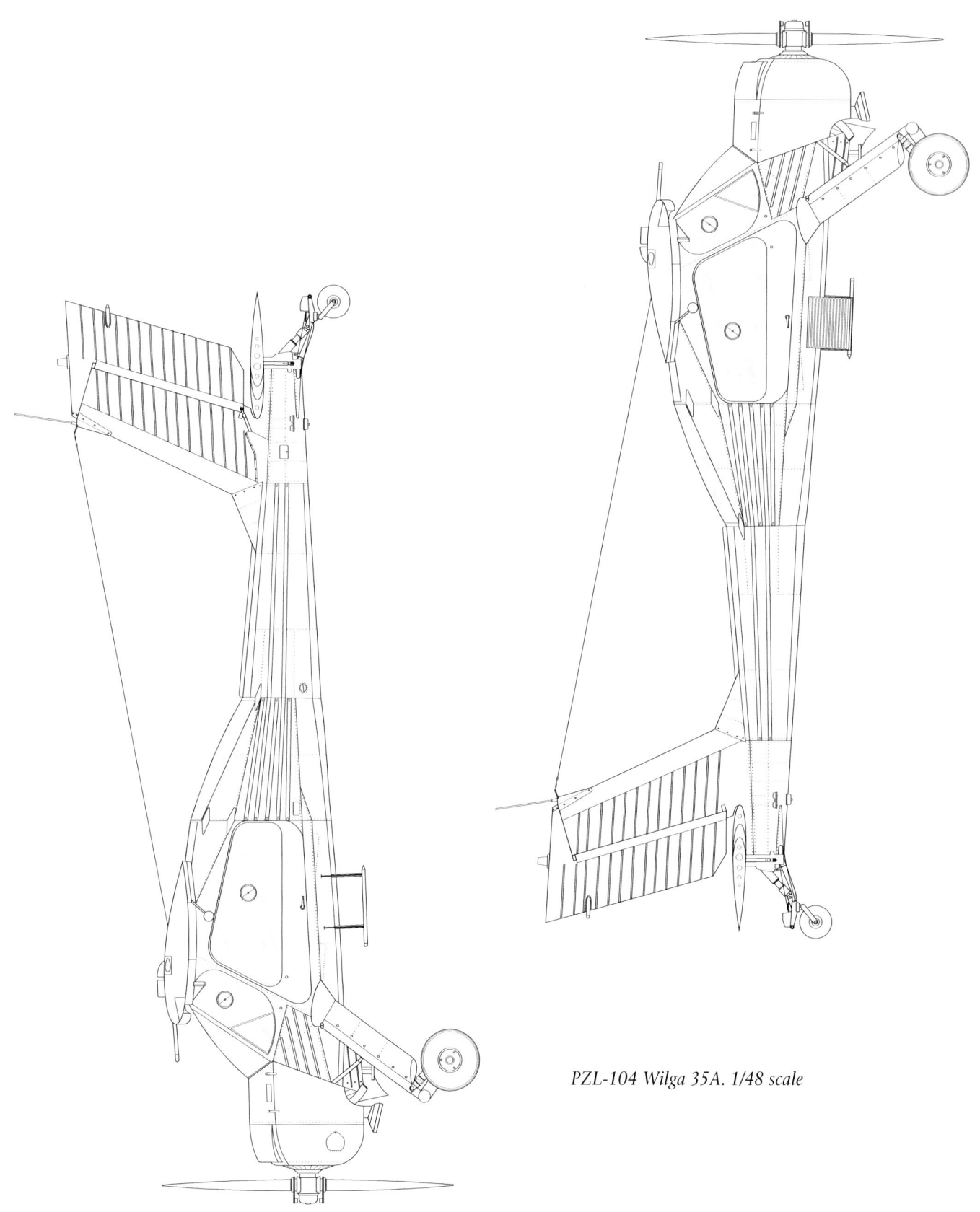

PZL-104 Wilga 35A. 1/48 scale

1/48

Drawings: Dariusz Karnas

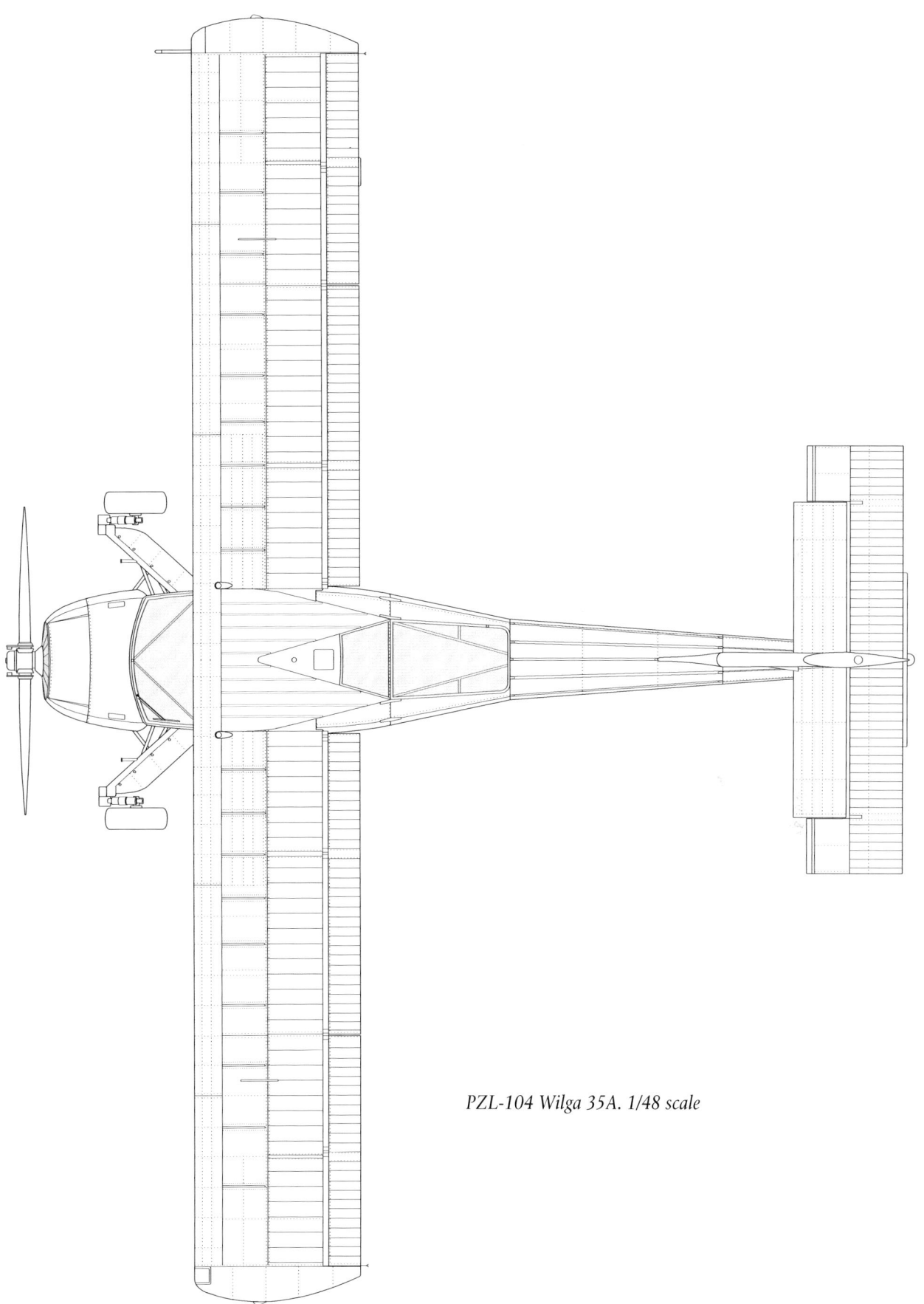

PZL-104 Wilga 35A. 1/48 scale

1/48

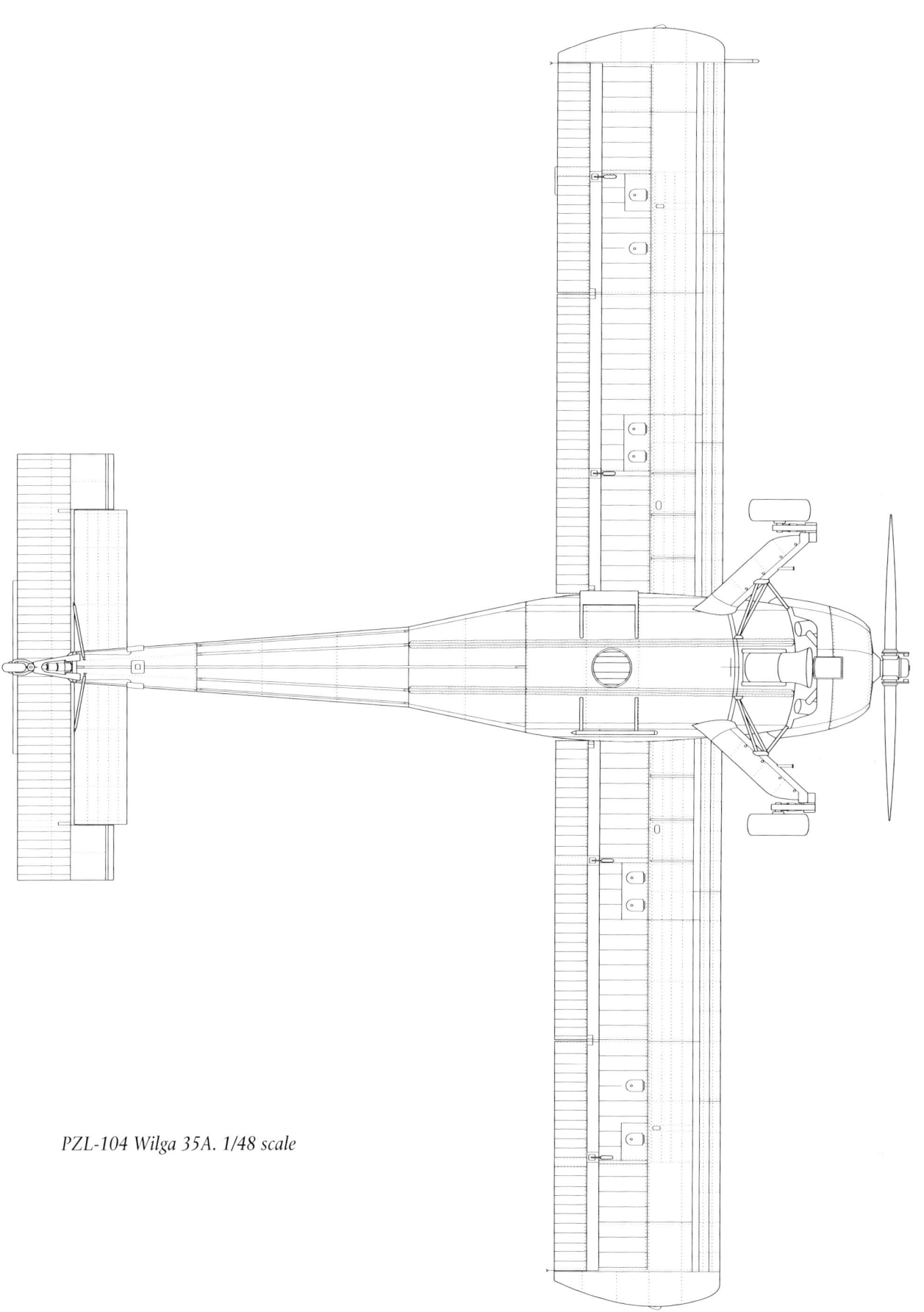

PZL-104 Wilga 35A. 1/48 scale

1/48

4

Drawings: Dariusz Karnas

PZL-104 Wilga 35A SP-CRS, serial number 17830690, belonging to the Stalowowolski Aeroclub, during maintenance work on the AI-14RA engine.

PZL-104 Wilga 35A SP-CRS of the Stalowowolski Aeroclub. (Both Dariusz Karnas)

Front windshield seen from the left side. Cabin vents clearly visible. (Dariusz Karnas)

Left main landing gear with the cover removed. (Dariusz Karnas)

Details of the AI-14 engine, view from the left and right side of the aircraft. (Miłosz Rusiecki)

Interior of the cockpit. The open battery hatch is visible. (Miłosz Rusiecki)

Internal structure of the lower part of the fuselage. (Miłosz Rusiecki)

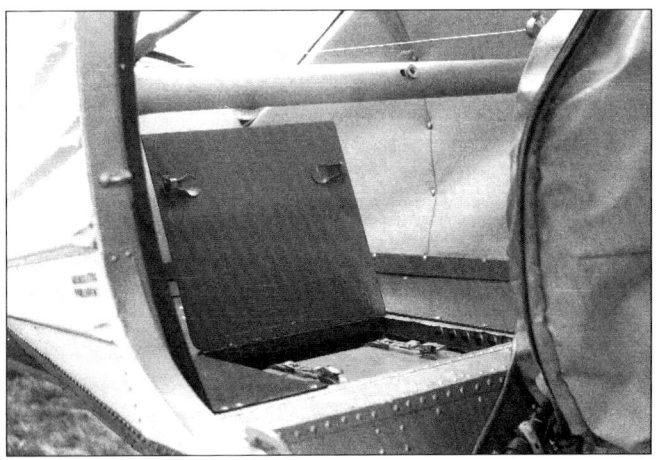

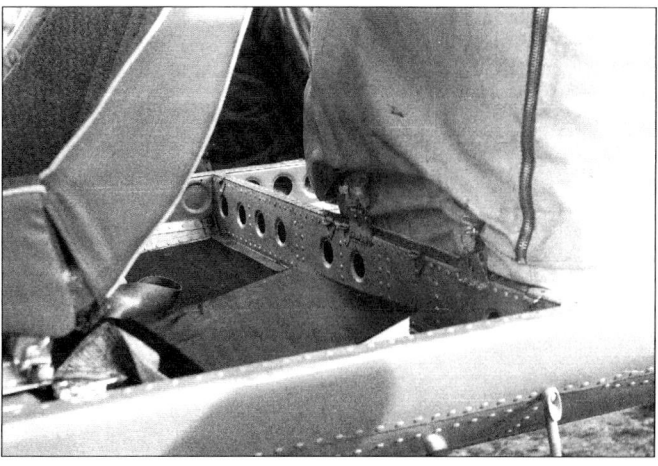

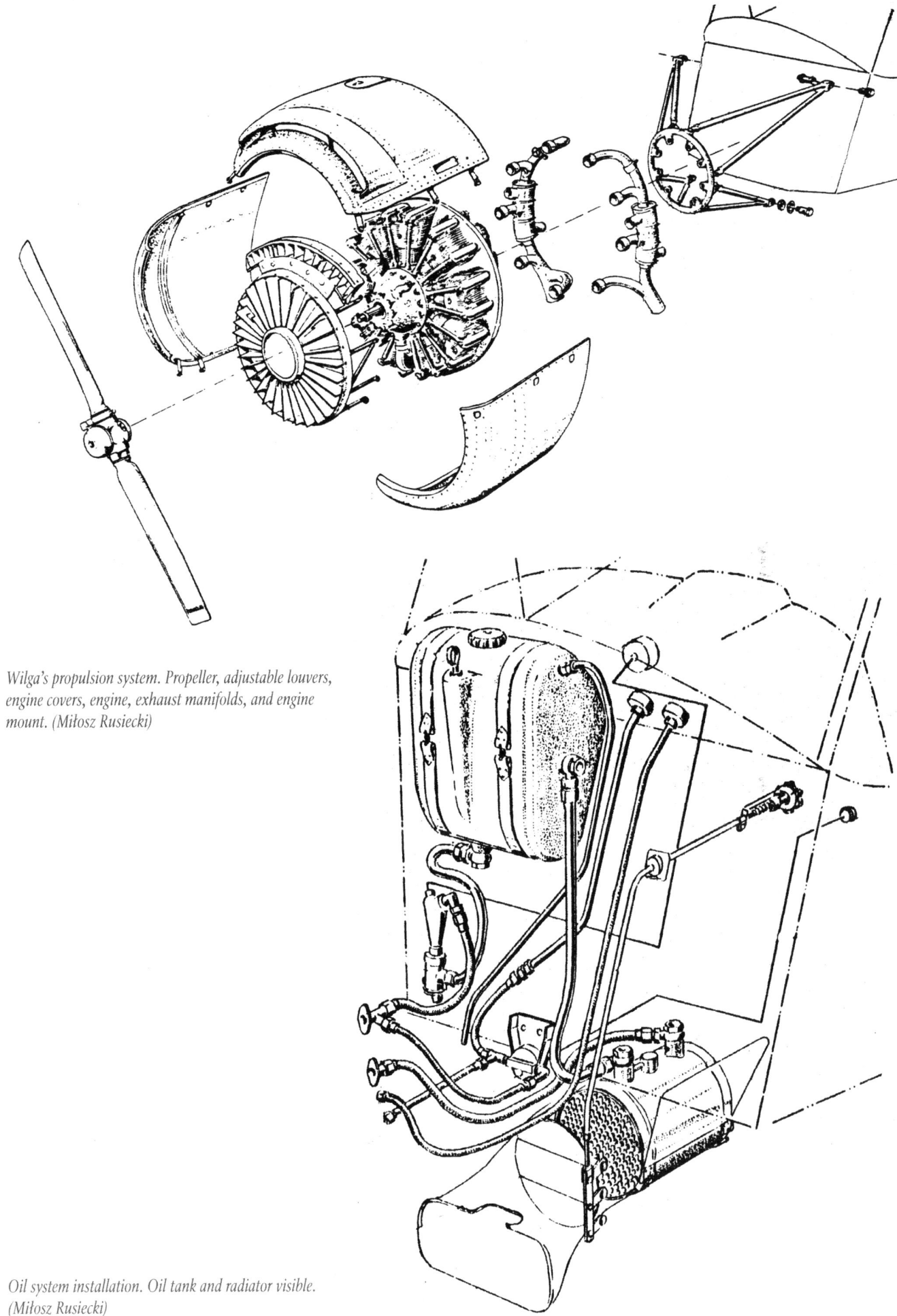

Wilga's propulsion system. Propeller, adjustable louvers, engine covers, engine, exhaust manifolds, and engine mount. (Miłosz Rusiecki)

Oil system installation. Oil tank and radiator visible. (Miłosz Rusiecki)

Wilga's cockpit interior. The typical dual control system for this aircraft is visible, along with the instrument panel, control panel with the RS 6102 radio station and radio compass, seat mounts, rear window, and upholstery. (Dariusz Karnas, Miłosz Rusiecki)

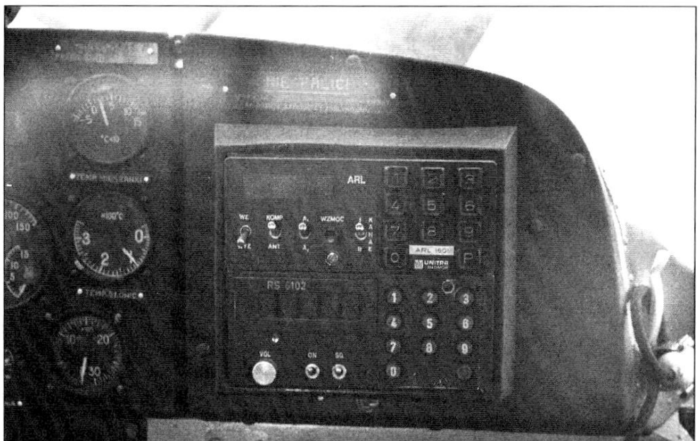

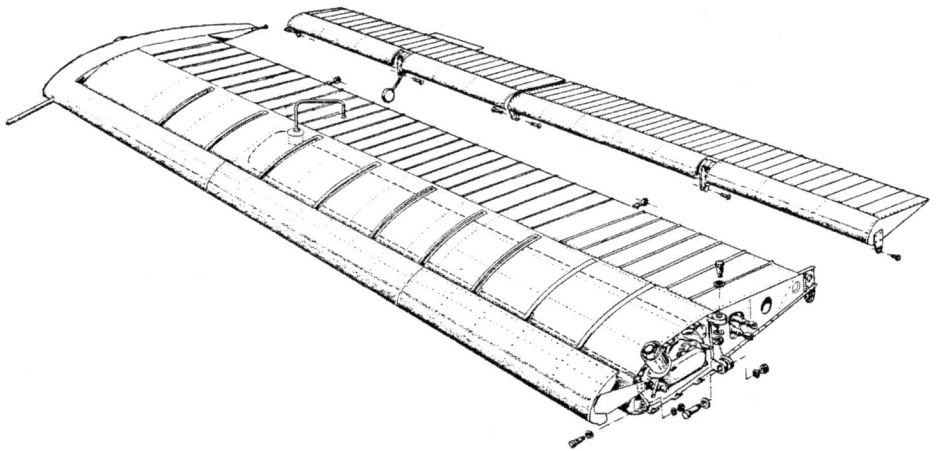

1. Engine start button
2. Ignition switch
3. Fuel shut-off valve
4. Altitude correction control
5. Primer pump
6. Headlight switch
7. Control knob for the louver blinds
8. Control knob for the oil cooler shutter
9. Airspeed indicator
10. Altimeter
11. Gyroscopic compass heading indicator
12. Artificial horizon
13. Vertical speed indicator (VSI) or variometer
14. Tachometer
15. Cylinder head temperature gauge
16. Engine controller
17. Manifold pressure gauge (supercharger pressure)
18. Carburetor air temperature gauge
19. Ammeter or voltmeter
20. Compass
21. Instrument correction plates
22. Portable lamp socket
23. Portable radio station socket

Wing with aileron and flap. Fuel tank in the wing box.

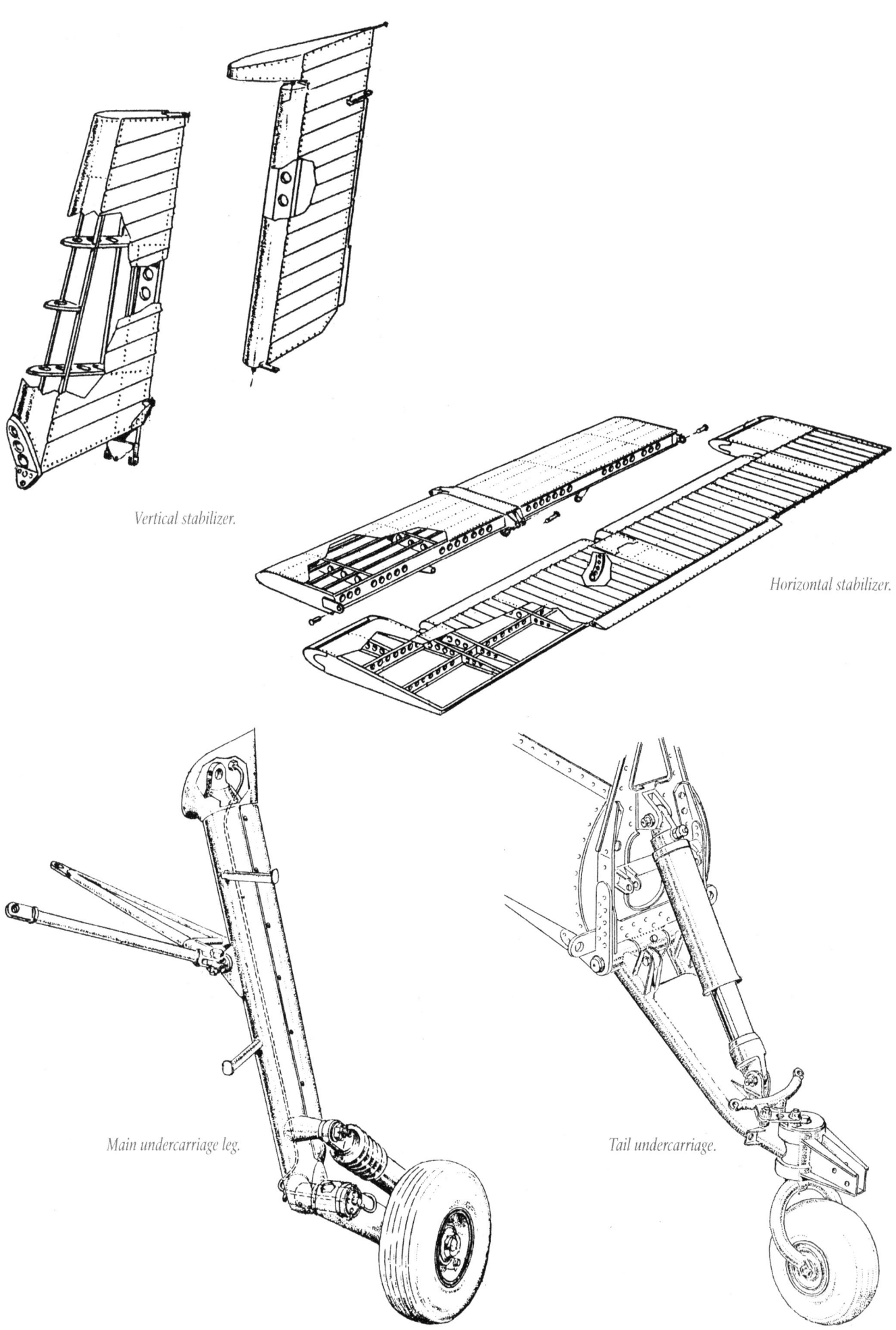

Vertical stabilizer.

Horizontal stabilizer.

Main undercarriage leg.

Tail undercarriage.

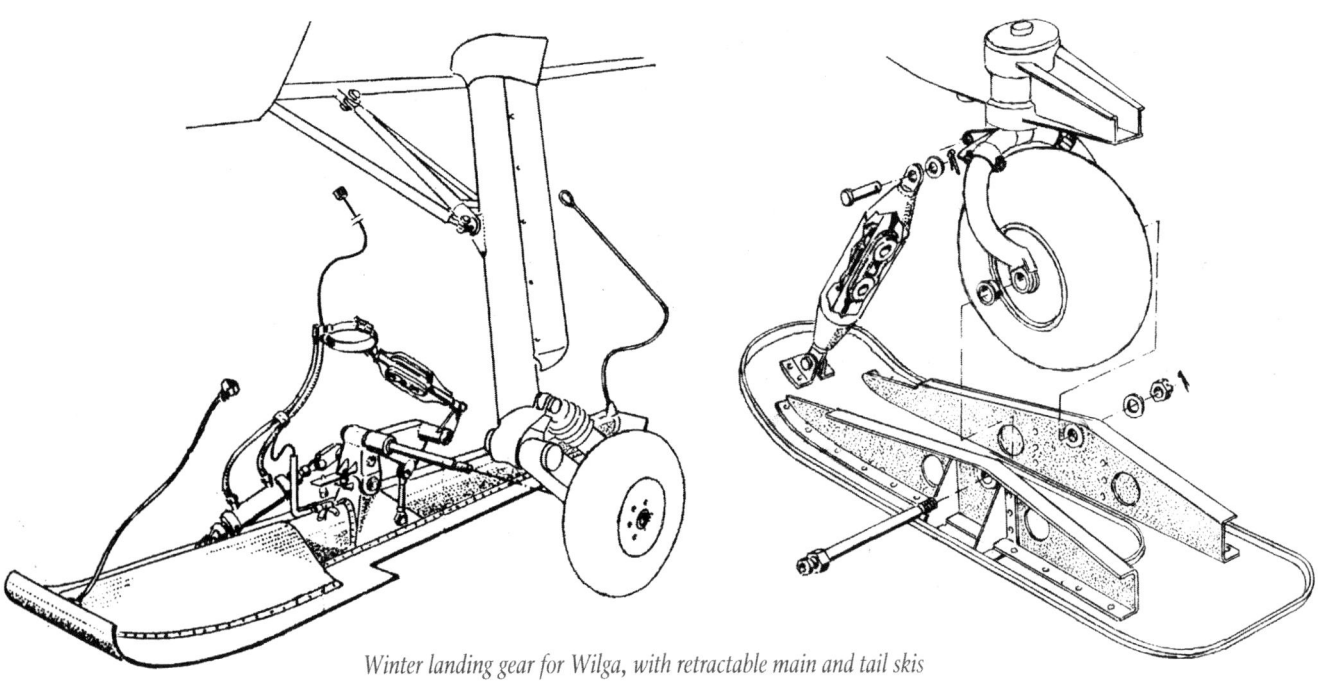

Winter landing gear for Wilga, with retractable main and tail skis

Mufflers characteristic of PZL-104 Wilga 80.

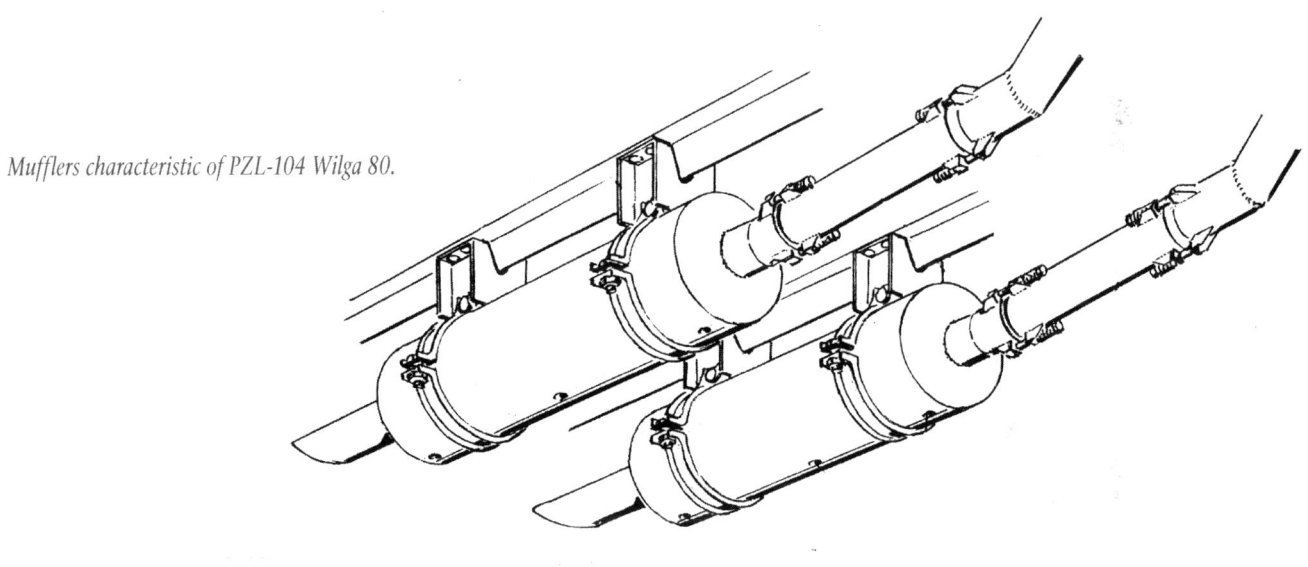

Control system for ailerons and flaps.

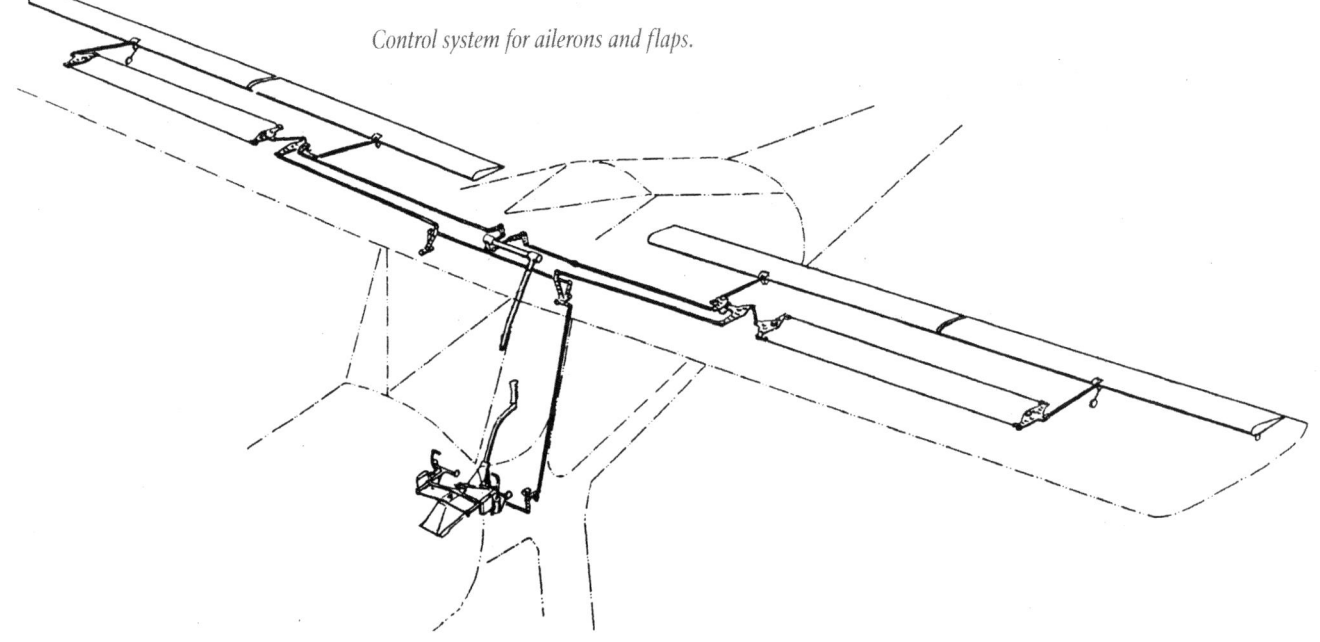

The characteristic silhouette of Wilga in a front view. The method of opening the cockpit doors is visible. (Dariusz Karnas)

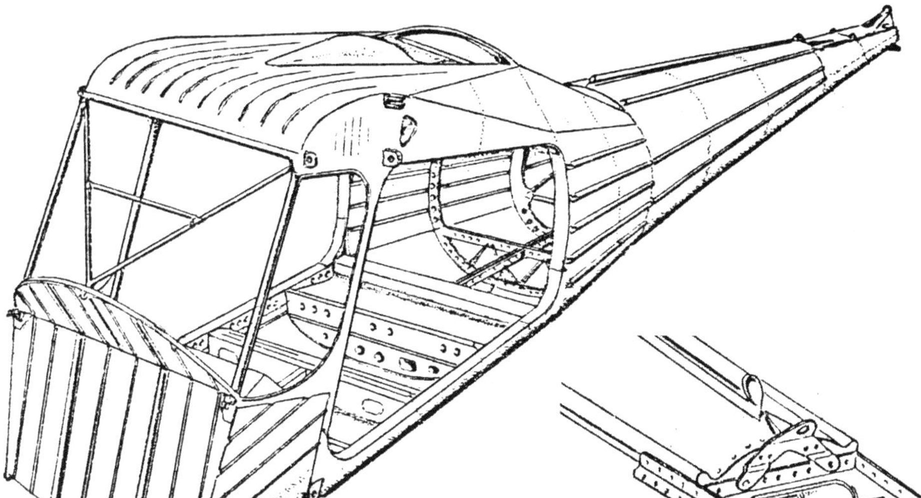

The structure of the front and rear parts of the fuselage.

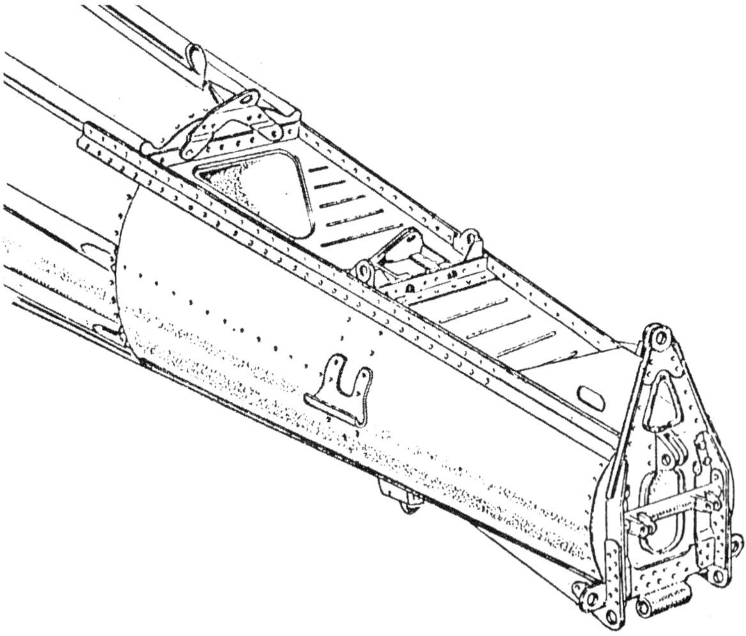

The engine with covers removed. The propeller hub with pitch adjustment elements is visible. (Piotr Strzeleck)

Engine cowling of the Wilga aircraft with the oil filler inspection window visible.

Right main landing gear strut mounts. (Dariusz Karnas.)

Stencils „TU PODPIERAĆ" and „ŁADOWANIE POWIETRZA"

Tailwheel. (Dariusz Karnas)

Main landing gear shock absorber and wheel - left strut. (Dariusz Karnas)

Right main landing gear with the removed aerodynamic fairing. (Dariusz Karnas)

Taiwheel. (Dariusz Karnas)

Landing light on the left wingtip. (Dariusz Karnas)

Inspection panels on the underside of the wing. (Dariusz Karnas)

Float-type fuel level indicator. (Dariusz Karnas)

The rear part of the Wilga fuselage. Visible structural reinforcement profiles and the rudder control system. (Dariusz Karnas)

View of the left and right side of the tail empennage. (Dariusz Karnas)

The aircraft PZL-104 Wilga 35A, with serial number 19850823 and registration marks SP-AGW, was manufactured on March 27, 1985. Originally, it had the red and white livery characteristic of Wilga aircraft. In 1986, Wacław Nycz from Aeroklub Rzeszowski won the 1st place in the II International Aircraft Precision Flying Championships held in Dubnica, former Czechoslovakia, flying SP-AGW.
In 1990, the aircraft underwent a major overhaul at the Aircraft Production and Repair Plant in Krosno, during which it received a new paint job. The plan was to decorate SP-AGW with a painting identifying the aircraft with Kraków, featuring a peacock feather as an ornament inspired by the traditional "krakuska" cap. However, problems with obtaining the appropriate paints prevented the complete execution of the design. As a result, on May 31, 1991, the Wilga was painted with light blue paint and flown by Tadeusz Wesołowski to the Aeroklub Krakowski airfield in Pobiednik Wielki.
The distinctive peacock feathers were finally painted on the aircraft in 1992 by the author of the design, a well-known artist named Marek Radomski.
(Marek Radomski)

PZL-104 Wilga 35A SP-AGW in its final painting at the Aeroklub Krakowski airfield. (Marek Radomski)

The elements of SP-AGW's paint job.
(Marek Radomski)

After the end of its service in the aeroclub, Wilga SP-AGW was transferred to the "Muzeum Narodowego Rolnictwa i Przemysłu Rolno Spożywczego" in Szreniawa near Poznań in December 2011. There, the aircraft was transformed into an agricultural version. It received a dummy underbelly tank for chemicals and appropriately adapted Agro equipment from a PZL-106 Kruk aircraft. Additionally, the rear seats were removed, and a 90-liter fuel tank was installed in their place. (Miłosz Rusiecki)

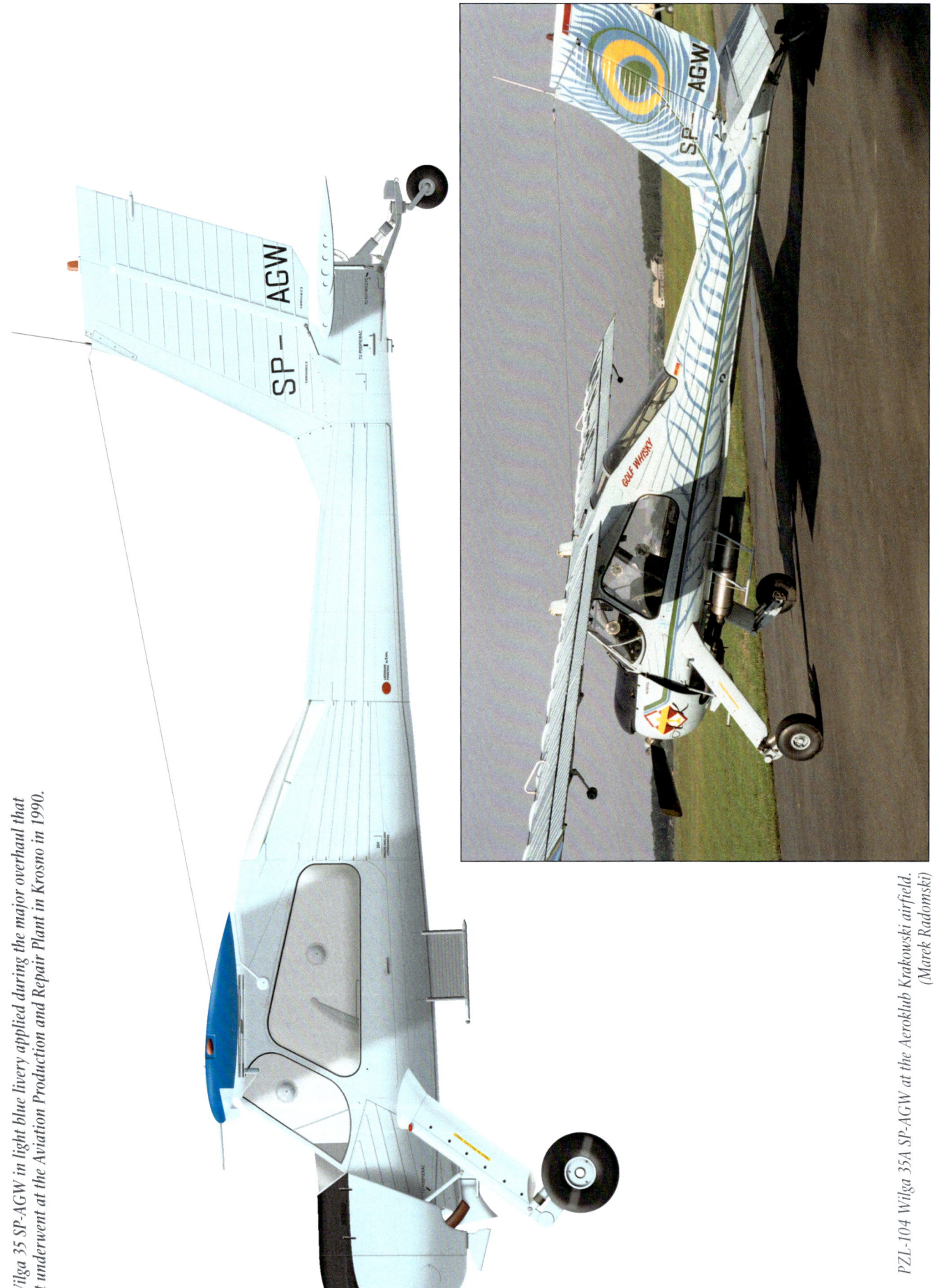

PZL-104 Wilga 35 SP-AGW in light blue livery applied during the major overhaul that the aircraft underwent at the Aviation Production and Repair Plant in Krosno in 1990.

PZL-104 Wilga 35A SP-AGW at the Aeroklub Krakowski airfield.
(Marek Radomski)

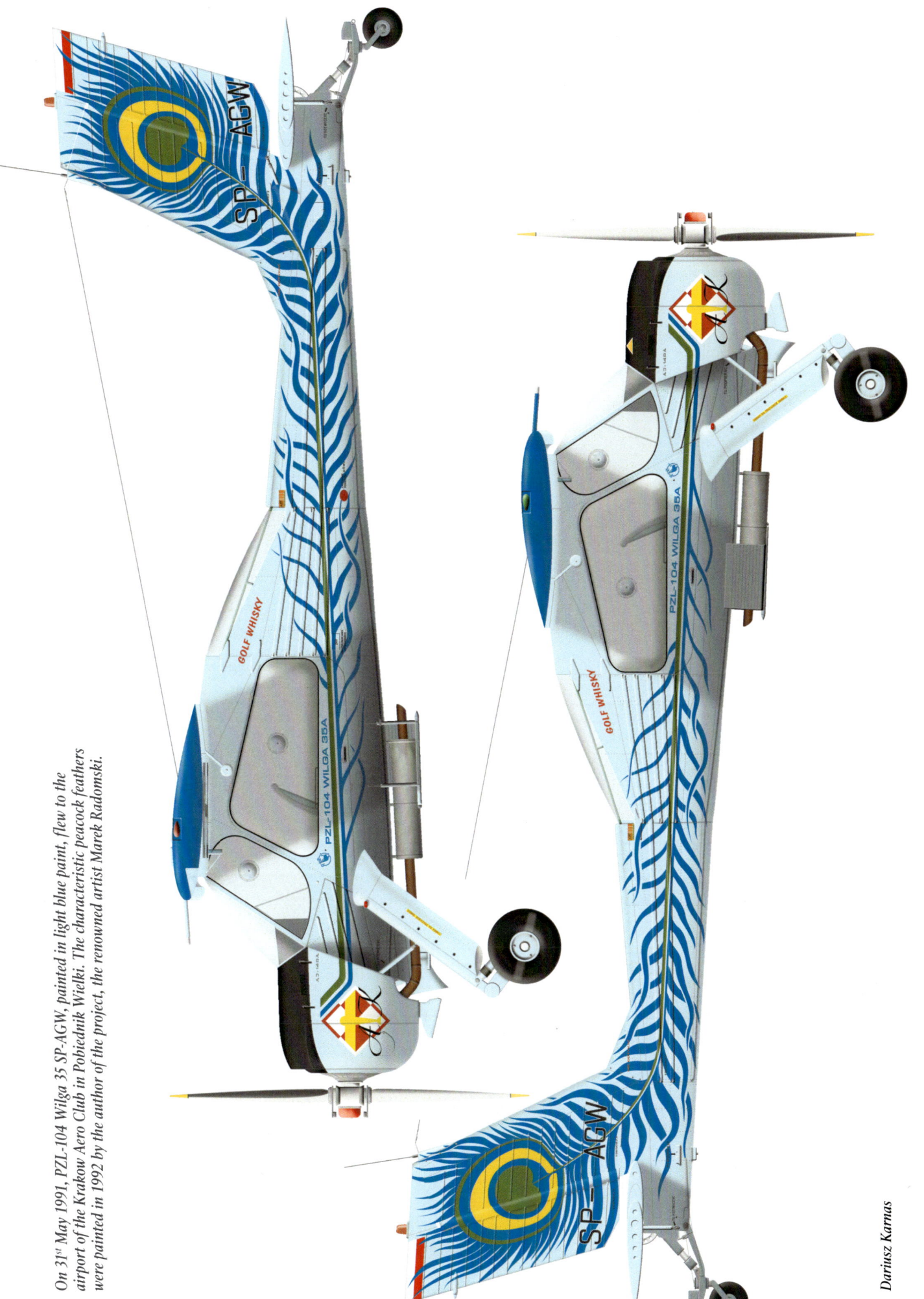

On 31st May 1991, PZL-104 Wilga 35 SP-AGW, painted in light blue paint, flew to the airport of the Krakow Aero Club in Pobiednik Wielki. The characteristic peacock feathers were painted in 1992 by the author of the project, the renowned artist Marek Radomski.

Dariusz Karnas

23

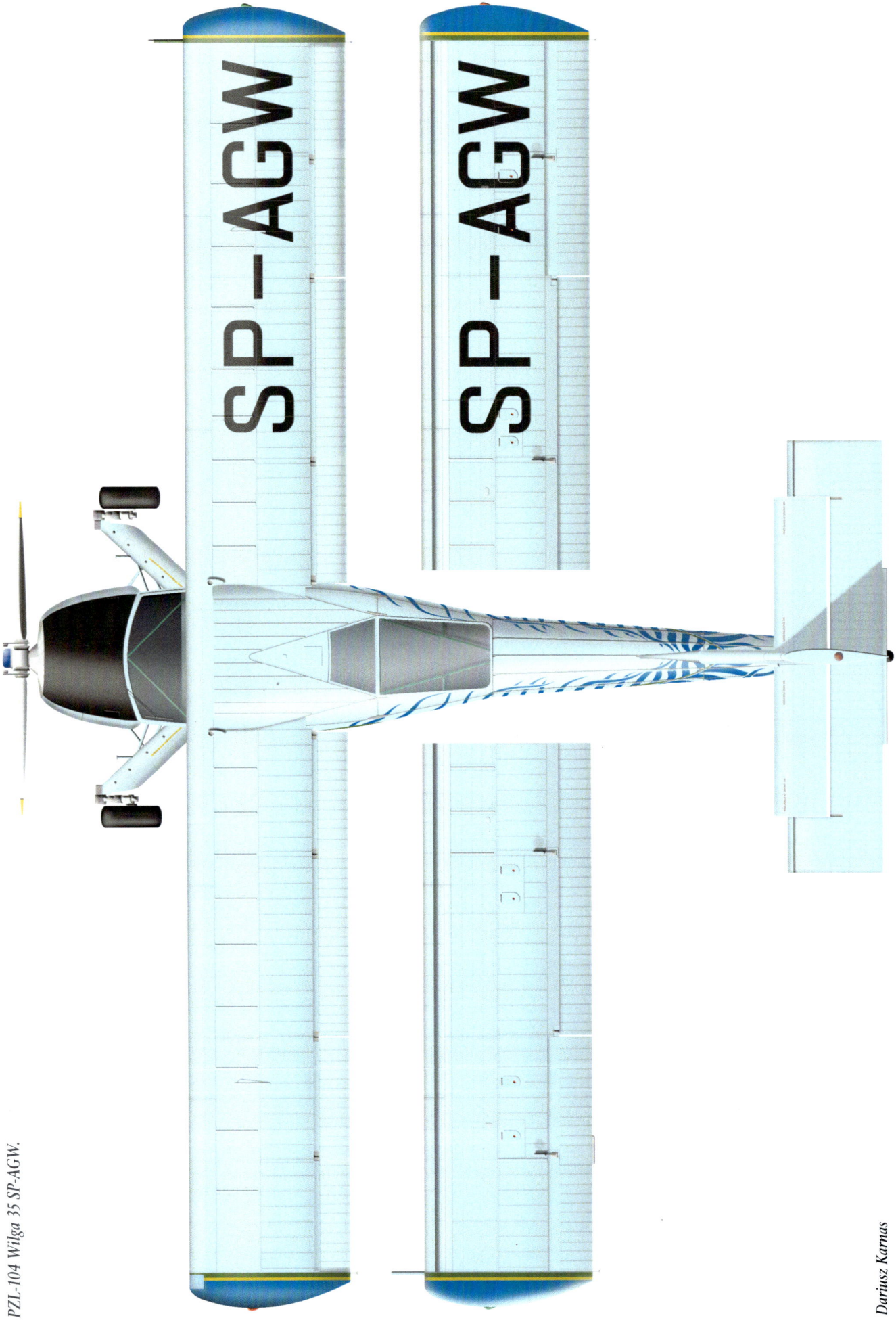

Dariusz Karnas